COLLINS AURA GARDEN HANDBOOKS

COLOUR
THROUGH THE YEAR

ALAN TOOGOOD

COLLINS

Editors Maggie Daykin, Susanne Mitchell
Designer Chris Walker
Picture research Moira McIlroy

First published 1988 by
William Collins Sons & Co Ltd
London · Glasgow · Sydney
Auckland · Toronto · Johannesburg

© Marshall Cavendish Limited 1988

British Library Cataloguing in Publication Data

Toogood, Alan R.

Colour through the year. —— (Collins Aura
    garden handbooks).
    1. Colour in gardening —— Great Britain
    I. Title
    712′.6′0941   SB454.C64

    ISBN 0–00–412390–5

Photoset by Bookworm Typesetting
Printed and bound in Hong Kong by Dai Nippon Printing
Company

Front cover: Garden scene by Pat Brindley
Back cover: Woodland scene by Michael Warren

CONTENTS

Introduction   4
Basic Colour Planning   8
Creating Illusions   12
One-colour Gardens   14
Foliage for Colour   20
Colourful Stems   24
Berries and Fruits   28
Other Forms of Colour   32
Seasonal Colour   36
Index and Acknowledgements   48

INTRODUCTION

Many home owners spend some considerable time planning interior colour schemes, yet I wonder if they give as much thought to colour in the garden. There is a certain amount of general information available on this subject but this little volume is somewhat unique in that it embraces all the basic principles of colour planning and gives many familiar and more unusual ideas for using colour.

Pink roses and silver-leaved perennials create a warm yet restful mood in this garden and are well set off by a deep green hedge.

Planning colour schemes for the garden is not as difficult as it can sometimes be indoors, where we are particularly careful to avoid violent clashes of colour. We aim for colours which harmonise and complement each other.

It is said that in nature few colours clash and I have found this to be largely true, though there is no logical explanation for it. There is consequently far less likelihood of making disastrous mistakes in the garden than in the home. Some bi-coloured flowers, for instance, contain colours such as orange and pink that we would find difficult to combine successfully in interior colour schemes.

As in the home, colour establishes the mood of the garden and reflects the owner's taste. When you plan a garden for colour you are making a personal statement for all to see – at least in your front garden.

Generally, you would be well advised to stick to a scheme when it comes to colour. For instance, your house may call for a cottagey garden, full of flowers and plants of all colours. Or you may feel that restrained use of colour would be more in keeping.

There is no reason why you should not use just two or three colours. If, for instance, you want to create a warm atmosphere, you could plan for

6

beds and borders mainly in shades of red and purple. Mainly pink schemes would also create a warm mood. To evoke a bright, cheerful sunshine mood, yellow flowers and foliage would be the answer.

You may perhaps want to create a cool atmosphere. If so, try a green and white planting scheme; or for a really cool effect use blue flowers and silver or grey foliage plants. Personally I would consider this to be more suitable for a warmer climate than ours – but the choice is up to you as there are few hard and fast rules in colour planning.

Of course, you don't have to plan the entire garden this way, particularly if it is large and can be divided with screens, hedges and so on, so that it is not all seen at one glance. You could then have different colour schemes in various parts of the garden. This approach can be seen in the Hidcote garden in Gloucestershire, where there is a green and white garden, and a border planted with red flowering and foliage plants.

To create a cool atmosphere try a green and white planting scheme. Here, some golden foliage has been included too, such as the grass-like carex.

A bright, cheerful, sunshine mood created with mainly yellow marigolds.

BASIC COLOUR PLANNING

Most gardens need a permanent living framework to give them an established look. This framework is green – the basic colour of most gardens. It is formed of lawns, possibly hedges, and permanent plants, mainly shrubs and trees. Other colours are provided by less permanent plants in beds and borders, and perhaps in tubs and other containers.

LEFT Green is the basic colour of gardens and provides the perfect background for other colours, such as the brilliant flame shades of autumn leaves.

RIGHT Pale colours can be used to separate strong and clashing colours. Here, white and pale pink astilbes have been used to good effect

Do not be concerned that this green framework will be dull, for there are many shades of green, of which I would suggest you use as many as possible. There are light, medium and deep greens, blue-greens, grey-greens, bronze-greens, silver-greens and yellow-greens. Just look at plants in a garden centre and you will see what I mean – particularly the conifers and the foliage shrubs.

This green framework provides a marvellous background for bright colours. Indeed, suitable backgrounds are vital, for they ensure that colours show to best advantage rather than simply merging into the general landscape.

For example, a border of colourful flowering perennial plants or annuals could be backed by a deep green hedge, such as yew, holly, or a dark form of Lawson cypress such as 'Green Hedger'. A bed of roses would benefit from a similar background.

Trees and shrubs noted for their autumn leaf colour or bright berries certainly show up best against deep green evergreen shrubs or trees. In winter, flowering shrubs such as witch hazel, winter sweet, winter-flowering cherry and viburnums need the same type of background or their flowers will simply not show up. Shrubs and trees with coloured stems or bark, like the birches, come into their own in the winter but must have a solid deep green background, provided by conifers and evergreen shrubs like laurustinus or rhododendrons.

Complementary colours As I have mentioned in my introduction, in nature few colours clash, but I would not attempt to combine some, such as orange and pink, or orange and lilac or mauve shades. I would also be very careful with really strong yellows and reds as combinations can be over-powering.

However, many people will want these colours in their gardens, perhaps even in the same bed or border. If the plants flower at the same time, try to keep them well apart, or separate them with pale or neutral colours such as white or cream. White, I find, is most useful for separating groupings of plants in strong, clashing colours as it goes with anything.

Another solution is to choose plants which flower at different times of the year if you need to grow them close together.

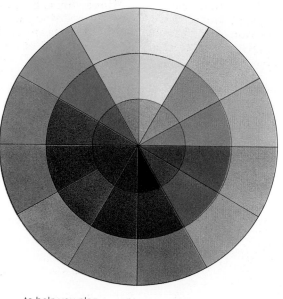

The colour wheel comprises the three primary colours – red, blue and yellow – with the intermediate colours, obtained by mixing the primary colours, between them. Use this wheel to help you plan harmonizing and contrasting colour schemes. Complementary colours face each other and the closer the colours the better they harmonize.

The aim should be to combine plants with contrasting or harmonizing colours. How do we know which colours complement each other? Be guided by a colour wheel (see accompanying drawing). This comprises the three primary colours – red, blue and yellow – with the intermediate colours, obtained by mixing the primary colours, between them. On this wheel all the complementary colours face each other – red, for example, complements green, blue complements orange, yellow complements violet, and so on.

The closer the colours on this wheel the better they harmonize. What are the differences between contrasting and harmonizing colours? Basically contrasting colours create a more dramatic effect even violent in some instances, as with blue and orange. Harmonizing colours create a more subtle and restful atmosphere.

I have already suggested on page 6 how you could limit colours in a garden. But how do you handle many colours in one border? Well, you could arrange them in a progressive sequence, along the length of the border. Start at one end with white and pale yellow, and progress to stronger colours like the oranges, reds, scarlets and crimsons. This gives a rainbow effect which many people find very pleasing.

It probably goes without saying, but when you are grouping plants together for particular colour effects you must be sure they all flower at the same time. Foliage plants, however, have a very long season of interest, so there is generally no problem with them.

Consider the site When colour planning, do take your garden's location into consideration. If, for instance, it is in a wild, rugged part of the country impressive for its natural beauty, you may not want to fill it with a mass of riotous colour. On the other hand, if you live in a 'concrete jungle', then this highly colourful approach might be welcome.

Plants must be chosen to suit the aspect, too. Many of the gold and silver foliage plants, and many flowers, need full sun. Yet equally many colourful plants will thrive in shade. Suitable aspects are indicated in the plant lists included later in the book, together with the soils they like, which are equally important. Some plants need moist soil while others need it well-drained. When grouping different kinds of plants together make sure they are all suited to the particular aspect and soil conditions that are available.

LEFT A well-planned mixed border with harmonizing and contrasting colours. It also blends in perfectly well with the countryside seen just beyond.

BELOW A good, harmonious border comprising mainly shades of green and gold. Many of the gold-foliage plants need full sun.

CREATING ILLUSIONS

Colours can be used to create illusions in a garden. They can be used to make some gardens look larger, others smaller or wider; or to make borders look longer or shorter. The principle is that pale colours can create a sense of distance because they are not seen so intensely, while strong bright colours, which are more clearly seen, seem to be nearer to the eye and can therefore appear to bring parts of a garden closer.

If, for example, you want to make a border appear longer than it really is, then start at the far end – furthest from the house – with pale colours, such as greys, silver, very pale blues or mauves, very pale greens, and so on. Then at the end nearest the house use very strong colours, such as reds, oranges, scarlet, crimson, very dark blues and purple. If you want to make a border appear shorter, simply reverse the colours – strong ones at the far end, pale ones near the house.

This principle can also be used to make a garden appear wider than it really is. Try a border of pale colours on one side and a border of strong colours on the other.

Mirror images help create an illusion of width too. If, for instance, you plant a golden-foliage shrub, such as *Philadelphus coronarius* 'Aureus' or the conifer *Chamaecyparis lawsoniana* 'Lanei', on one side of the garden, plant another exactly opposite on the other side.

To prevent a closed-in feeling when planting boundary hedges in small gardens, go for light-coloured hedging plants rather than those with deep green foliage. Use golden privet rather than green, for example, or a pale grey variety of Lawson cypress instead of the normal dark green hedging type.

If you plant very pale-coloured trees or shrubs at the end of a garden – perhaps in a lawn – the garden will look much longer than it really is. Suitable trees would be the willow-leaved pear, *Pyrus salicifolia* 'Pendula', or the grey conifers such as *Chamaecyparis lawsoniana* 'Columnaris'. Stronger-coloured trees or shrubs could then be planted nearer the house, such as purple-leaved *Cotinus coggygria* 'Royal Purple' or golden-leaved *Gleditsia triacanthos* 'Sunburst'.

You can not only use plants to create such illusions, but also pale

statuary, urns and vases in white, grey or beige. They can form focal points, say at the end of a lawn, and also create a sense of distance.

The same applies to any artificial screen put up in the garden, such as trelliswork or screen-block walling. The latter comes in pale or neutral colours anyway, but not so trellis, though it could be painted white or very pale grey.

Containers near the house, on a patio or terrace, can be strongly coloured – terracotta, or dark oak if it is a barrel or wooden tub – and planted with flowers in bright strong colours.

LEFT Pale colours at the far end of a border, with strong colours at the near end, will make the border appear longer than it really is.

RIGHT A pale focal point at the end of a vista, such as a white seat, will create a sense of distance.

ONE-COLOUR GARDENS

Single-colour schemes can be a novel and exciting way of displaying plants. But you do not have to devote an entire garden, border or bed to a single colour, though this could be most impressive. You could try out a scheme in a small bed or part of a border. Besides using flowering plants, include some with coloured foliage, berries and stems. Here I will recommend only flowering plants. You will discover foliage, berries and stems mentioned later in the book.

To create a cool atmosphere, try a blue border using blue-flowered perennials, shrubs and other plants.

A red scheme This will create a warm mood in a garden and is particularly cheerful on dull days, of which we seem to have many when the garden is most often used in summer. You could include purple foliage plants in a red scheme, as well as plants with red-violet, violet, orange-red and orange flowers. A completely red garden could be overdone, so you might consider instead a red border or bed in a part of the garden that needs brightening up.

Many plants have red flowers. Some of the 'essential' ones, which need sun and well-drained soil unless otherwise stated, are listed here.

PERENNIALS FOR SPRING OR EARLY SUMMER *Bergenia* 'Ballawley' (moist soil and shade), Lupin 'The Pages', *Paeonia lactiflora* 'Felix Crousse' and *Papaver orientale* 'Ladybird'.

PERENNIALS FOR SUMMER *Astilbe* 'Fanal' (moist soil and light shade), dianthus (carnations and pinks), *Euphorbia griffithii* 'Fireglow', *Geum* 'Mrs Bradshaw', *Lobelia cardinalis* (moist soil and light shade), *Lychnis chalcedonica* and *Phlox paniculata* 'Red Indian' (moist soil).

RED GROUPS
Spring: tulips interplanted with polyanthus.
Summer: dahlias with shrub roses, purple delphiniums, and a backing of the purple-leaved shrub *Cotinus coggygria* 'Royal Purple'.
Autumn: asters (Michaelmas daisies) behind a group of *Spiraea × bumalda* 'Anthony Waterer' (still in flower); with frontal groups of schizostylis.

PERENNIALS FOR AUTUMN *Aster novi-belgii* 'Winston S. Churchill'.

SHRUBS FOR SPRING *Ribes sanguineum* 'Pulborough Scarlet'.

SHRUBS FOR SUMMER *Cistus × purpureus, Escallonia* 'Crimson Spire', *Hydrangea macrophylla* 'Ami Pasquier' (needs moist soil and light shade), shrub rose 'Heidelberg', *Spiraea × bumalda* 'Anthony Waterer' and *Weigela* 'Bristol Ruby'.

BEDDING PLANTS FOR SPRING polyanthus 'Crimson King' (needs moist soil, takes shade).

BEDDING PLANTS AND ANNUALS FOR SUMMER *Begonia semperflorens* 'Danica Red' (likes moist soil and light shade), *Dianthus barbatus* 'Crimson Velvet', *Impatiens* 'Blitz' (likes moist soil and light shade), *Pelargonium* 'Mustang' (seed raised), *Petunia* 'Red Joy', *Salvia splendens* 'Fireball' and *Verbena* 'Blaze'.

BULBS *Dahlia* 'Bacchus' (summer), *Gladiolus* 'Carmen' (summer), *Schizostylis coccinea* 'Major' (autumn) and tulip 'Red Riding Hood' (spring).

White and green scheme Using white-flowered plants, and plants with green blooms, as well as foliage plants with plain green or green and white variegated leaves, will create a very cool, tranquil atmosphere. Shady corners often look good planted with green and white plants of which several suitable kinds are listed here. Don't forget to include variegated hostas and some ferns in shady moist spots.

A selection of white-flowered plants follows. Unless otherwise stated, all of these plants need a sunny spot and well-drained soil.

The lady's mantle or alchemilla, with its tiny, lime-green flowers, is a favourite plant for green and white schemes.

WHITE AND GREEN GROUPS
Spring: a carpet of *Erica carnea* 'Springwood White' around *Magnolia stellata*.
Summer: generous groups of *Alchemilla mollis* (lime-green flowers) combined with hostas with green and white variegated foliage.
Summer: *Phlox paniculata* 'White Admiral' next to the white and green striped grass, *Phalaris arundinacea* 'Picta'.

PERENNIALS FOR SPRING *Arabis caucasica* 'Plena', *Bergenia* 'Silberlicht' (moist soil, shade), *Dicentra spectabilis* 'Alba' (moist soil, shade), *Helleborus corsicus* (moist soil, shade), *Iberis* 'Snowflake'.

PERENNIALS FOR SUMMER *Alchemilla mollis* (lime green, moist soil, shade), *Anthemis cupaniana, Astilbe* 'Snowdrift' (moist soil), *Campanula latifolia* 'White Ladies' (moist soil), *Campanula persicifolia* 'Hampstead White' (moist soil), *Chrysanthemum maximum* 'Snowcap', *Cimicifuga racemosa* (moist soil), *Dianthus* 'Mrs Sinkins', *Gypsophila paniculata* 'Bristol Fairy', *Phlox paniculata* 'White Admiral' (moist soil), *Saxifraga fortunei* (moist soil, shade, autumn flowers), *Viola cornuta* 'Alba' (moist soil, shade).

SHRUBS FOR SPRING *Clematis montana* 'Alexander' (climber), *Erica carnea* 'Springwood White' (also winter), *Erica* × *darleyensis* 'Silberschmelze' (also winter), *Magnolia stellata, Spiraea nipponica tosaensis.*

Variegated and green-leaved hostas create a delightfully cool atmosphere in a shady spot and will thrive there. Good border plants if in partial shade.

SHRUBS FOR SUMMER *Calluna vulgaris* 'Mair's Variety' (acid soil), *Choisya ternata, Escallonia* 'Iveyi', *Philadelphus* 'Virginal', *Potentilla dahurica* 'Manchu', *Viburnum opulus* 'Sterile'.

BULBS FOR SPRING AND SUMMER *Anemone blanda* 'Alba' (shade), *Galtonia candicans* (takes some shade), *Lilium* 'Green Dragon', *Narcissus* 'Mount Hood', *Ornithogalum umbellatum*, tulip 'White Triumphator'.

ANNUALS AND BEDDING FOR SUMMER *Alyssum* 'Snowdrift', *Euphorbia marginata* (green and white), *Gypsophila* 'Covent Garden White', *Lavatera trimestris* 'Mont Blanc', *Molucella laevis* (green blooms), *Nicotiana* 'Lime Green', *Petunia* 'White Joy', *Zinnia* 'Envy' (green).

Pink and silver scheme This is one of the favourite combinations – pink flowers and silver or grey foliage plants. It creates a delightful warm atmosphere in a garden but is more restful than a red bed or border. There are many pink-flowered plants to choose from and, again, unless otherwise stated, they like plenty of sun and well-drained soil. Silver foliage plants are on pages 22–3.

PINK AND SILVER GROUPS
Spring: *Bergenia* 'Pugsley's Pink' in front of the grey-leaved low-growing shrub *Senecio* 'Sunshine'.
Summer: border carnations or pinks with mats of silver-leaved *Stachys lanata* 'Silver Carpet'. Perhaps some groups, too, of the greyish dwarf grasses *Festuca glauca* and *Avena candida*.
Autumn: *Sedum spectabile* 'Autumn Joy' with *Stachys lanata* 'Silver Carpet'.

PERENNIALS Among those I can recommend for spring flowering are *Arabis caucasica* 'Rosabella' and, ideal for shade and moist soil, *Bergenia* 'Pugsley's Pink'.

There is no shortage of summer perennials and I would particularly recommend *Astilbe* 'Bressingham Beauty' (needs moist soil), dianthus or varieties of border carnations and pinks, *Geranium endressii* 'Wargrave Pink', *Hemerocallis* 'Pink Damask', *Paeonia lactiflora* 'Bowl of Beauty', *Phlox paniculata* 'Balmoral' (best in moist soil), and *Sidalcea* 'Loveliness'. For autumn try *Anemone × hybrida* 'September Charm', *Aster novi-belgii* 'Patricia Ballard' and the aptly-named *Sedum spectabile* 'Autumn Joy'.

A collection of silver-foliage plants, which need plenty of sun and combine well with yellow-flowered plants.

SHRUBS For spring these must include *Camellia × williamsii* 'Donation' and *Kolkwitzia amabilis*, while for summer no pink garden should be without *Cistus* 'Silver Pink', *Escallonia* 'Slieve Donard' and *Hebe* 'Carnea'.

BULBS AND BEDDING PLANTS I suggest for spring colour hyacinth 'Pink Pearl' and the pink Triumph Strain of polyanthus (ideal for moist shady conditions). For summer try *Allium cernuum*, *Antirrhinum* 'Leonard Sutton', *Aster* 'Milady Rose', *Begonia semperflorens* 'Frilly Pink' (suited to moist shade), *Cleome spinosa* 'Pink Queen', godetia, *Lavatera trimestris* 'Silver Cup' and *Petunia* 'Pink Joy'. Autumn bulbs must include *Colchicum speciosum* and *Nerine bowdenii*.

A yellow scheme For a bright sunny effect try a yellow scheme, but provide it with a dark background so that the foliage and flowers show up well. Incidentally, yellow flowers show up particularly well in the evening when the light is fading. Include some cream flowers, too, as well as plants with golden foliage. Grey-leaved plants also go well with yellow flowers and foliage and help create further interest.

Most of the plants in this list need sunny conditions and good drainage, but some are suited to shade and/or moist soils.

PERENNIALS FOR SPRING *Alyssum saxatile* 'Compactum', *Doronicum* 'Miss Mason', *Euphorbia epithymoides*, *Euphorbia sikkimensis*, *Trollius × hybridus* 'Canary Bird' (needs moist soil and partial shade).

PERENNIALS FOR SUMMER *Achillea* 'Coronation Gold', *Anthemis tinctoria* 'Mrs E.C. Buxton', *Artemisia lactiflora* (cream), *Aruncus sylvester* (cream, suitable for moist soil and light shade), *Coreopsis verticillata* 'Grandiflora', *Geum* 'Lady Stratheden', *Helenium* 'Butterpat', *Hemerocallis* 'Hyperion' (takes light shade), *Lysimachia punctata* (moist soil), *Oenothera missouriensis*, *Rudbeckia deamii*, *Solidago* 'Goldenmosa' (late flowering).

SHRUBS FOR SPRING *Cytisus × beanii, Cytisus × praecox* 'Allgold', *Forsythia* 'Lynwood', *Genista lydia, Kerria japonica* 'Pleniflora'.

SHRUBS FOR SUMMER *Hypericum* 'Hidcote', *Potentilla* 'Goldfinger', *Spartium junceum*.

SHRUBS FOR WINTER *Chimonanthus praecox, Mahonia* 'Charity'.

BULBS AND BEDDING FOR SPRING *Cheiranthus cheiri* 'Cloth of Gold' (wallflower), *Crocus chrysanthus* varieties, *Fritillaria imperialis* 'Lutea', *Narcissus* 'Carlton', Polyanthus 'Lemon Punch', Tulip 'Golden Harvest'.

BEDDING, ANNUALS AND BULBS FOR SUMMER *Allium moly* (ornamental onion), *Calendula* 'Lemon Queen', *Lilium* 'Destiny', *Limnanthes douglasii, Sternbergia lutea* (autumn), *Tagetes* 'Inca Yellow' (marigold), *Tropaeolum peregrinum* (climber), *Viola* (pansy) 'Golden Champion'.

YELLOW GROUPS
Spring: *Forsythia* 'Lynwood' as a background for grey-leaved *Senecio* 'Sunshine', and groups of yellow daffodils and polyanthus.
Summer: a background of golden-leaved shrub *Philadelphus coronarius* 'Aureus', with a group of *Aruncus sylvester* (cream flowers), and yellow-flowered *Coreopsis verticillata* 'Grandiflora' or *Achillea* 'Coronation Gold'.

Blue schemes To create a 'cool' atmosphere try a blue border, using blue-flowered perennials, shrubs, bulbs, annuals and bedding plants. Also include some white and cream flowers, not forgetting plenty of bluish or greyish foliage plants.

PERENNIALS There are plenty of these for the blue border: in winter there is *Iris unguicularis* followed, in spring, by *Brunnera macrophylla* and *Pulmonaria angustifolia*.

Genista cinerea (in the background) and the stately spikes of eremurus or foxtail lilies create a bright group in this mainly yellow border.

Delphiniums, in their many shades of blue, constitute for many people one of the major subjects for a mainly blue planting scheme. Lavender (front) is also indispensable.

Summer perennials should include *Aconitum napellus* 'Bressingham Spire', *Agapanthus* 'Headbourne Hybrids', *Anchusa azurea* 'Loddon Royalist', *Campanula lactiflora*, *Ceratostigma willmottianum* (flowers into autumn), *Cynoglossum nervosum* (takes light shade), *Delphinium* 'Pacific Hybrids', *Echinops ritro*, *Eryngium planum*, *Iris germanica* 'Patterdale', *Iris sibirica* 'Persimmon' (likes moist soil), *Meconopsis betonicifolia* (moist soil and light shade), and *Veronica gentianoides*.

SHRUBS FOR SPRING These include *Ceanothus* 'Delight', *Rhododendron augustinii* (acid soil), *Rhododendron scintillans* (acid soil), and the climber *Wisteria floribunda* 'Macrobotrys'.

SHRUBS FOR SUMMER Can include *Caryopteris × clandonensis* 'Heavenly Blue', *Hydrangea macrophylla* 'Blue Wave' (prefers a moist soil and shade), *Lavandula angustifolia* 'Grappenhall', *Perovskia atriplicifolia* 'Blue Spire' and *Rosmarinus officinalis*.

SPRING BULBS Almost essential are *Chionodoxa luciliae*, hyacinth 'Delft Blue' and *Muscari* 'Heavenly Blue'. These could be grown with spring-flowering *Myosotis* (forget-me-not) 'Royal Blue' (ideal for shade), and polyanthus Blue Triumph Strain (suitable for shade and moist soil).

SUMMER BEDDING PLANTS Recommended are *Ageratum* 'Blue Mink', *Lobelia* 'Cambridge Blue' and pansy 'Azure Blue'. With these could be included hardy annuals *Anchusa* 'Blue Angel', *Centaurea cyanus* (cornflower) 'Blue Diadem', *Ipomoea* 'Heavenly Blue' and *Salvia patens*.

BLUE GROUPS
Spring: a carpet of *Pulmonaria angustifolia* or *Brunnera macrophylla* with bulbs such as muscari growing around or through them.
Summer: *Delphinium* 'Pacific Hybrids' (blue) near a specimen of the small grey-leaved tree *Pyrus salicifolia* 'Pendula'. In front of these, groups of blue irises for early flowers and agapanthus for late blooms.
Summer: hostas with bluish or greyish foliage, like *H. sieboldiana* 'Elegans', with the blue poppy, *Meconopsis betonicifolia*. Ideal for a moist shady spot.

FOLIAGE FOR COLOUR

Do not think that colour depends exclusively on flowers. Foliage can also provide very pleasing colour and is often just as showy, possibly even more so, than many flowers. It has a very long season too – all the year round if you choose evergreens. I would suggest you do have a good sprinkling of evergreens, to make sure of winter interest. Perhaps some could be combined with winter-flowering shrubs and perennials.

Uses of foliage plants Foliage plants, whether shrubs, conifers, trees or perennials, can be combined with flowering and other foliage plants to create contrasts and harmonies. They are of particular value in one-colour schemes, but should also be included in every mixed bed or border. Some plants with more distinctive shapes, such as *Cupressus macrocarpa* 'Goldcrest', *Catalpa bignonioides* 'Aurea', *Robinia pseudoacacia* 'Frisia', and *Pyrus salicifolia* 'Pendula', make excellent specimen plants in a lawn.

I would suggest you do not overdo the use of large foliage plants in a general garden. Do not, for instance, plant coloured-leaved trees, shrubs and conifers to the exclusion of green-leaved kinds, or the effect could be rather overpowering. As I said earlier, the basic colour of a garden should be green. In a more natural country garden coloured-leaved trees and shrubs could look out of place, though small coloured-leaved plants, such as silver or grey perennials or variegated hostas, should blend in well enough.

Some coloured-foliage shrubs and trees can be used for hedging: such as *Prunus cerasifera* 'Nigra' (blackish-purple), *Berberis thunbergii* 'Atropurpurea' (reddish-purple), *Ligustrum ovalifolium* 'Aureum' (yellow), *Chamaecyparis lawsoniana* 'Lanei' (yellow), *Elaeagnus pungens* 'Maculata' (green and gold), *Ilex aquifolium* varieties (variegated), and lavender (grey) for a dwarf hedge.

Ideas for plant groups You could try the following simple but very effective schemes:
• Purple *Berberis* × *ottawensis* 'Purpurea' with red shrub roses.

LEFT There are many golden-foliage plants available like catalpa (background) and cone-shaped conifers.

RIGHT Green-leaved acers (background) here make a dramatic combination with orange *Euphorbia griffithii* 'Fireglow'.

- Variegated or golden hostas with candelabra primulas such as *P. japonica*.
- Variegated *Cornus alba* 'Elegantissima' with purple *Cotinus coggygria* 'Royal Purple'.
- The variegated grass, *Phalaris arundinacea* 'Picta' with varieties of border phlox (*P. paniculata*), especially those with strong colours.
- *Cotinus coggygria* 'Royal Purple' with the variegated grass *Phalaris arundinacea* 'Picta'.
- The grey-leaved tree, *Pyrus salicifolia* 'Pendula', surrounded by the red-flowered perennial, *Euphorbia griffithii* 'Fireglow'.

Sun or shade It is safe to say that most coloured foliage plants need plenty of sun. But some will still be effective in shade and these are indicated in the lists of plants.

Red-purple plants Will take shade for part of the day.

Golden plants Mostly need as much sun as possible, though some, such as many of the golden hostas, will retain their colour when planted in a shady spot.

Variegated plants Many of these are more tolerant of shade for much of the day than are the golden-leaved plants.

Silver/grey plants Great sun lovers, needing very well-drained soil.

Recommended plants In the following lists E indicates evergreen, and S means suitable for shade.

RED/PURPLE SHRUBS/TREES *Acer palmatum* 'Atropurpureum' (S), *Acer platanoides* 'Crimson King', *Berberis thunbergii* 'Atropurpurea', *Berberis thunbergii* 'Dart's Red Lady', *Berberis × ottawensis* 'Purpurea', *Corylus maxima* 'Purpurea', *Cotinus coggygria* 'Royal Purple', *Photinia × fraseri* 'Red Robin' (E,S), *Prunus cerasifera* 'Nigra', *Prunus × cistena*, *Salvia officinalis* 'Purpurascens' (E), *Vitis vinifera* 'Purpurea'.

GOLDEN SHRUBS/TREES *Acer japonicum* 'Aureum', *Berberis thunbergii* 'Aurea', *Calluna vulgaris* 'Gold Haze' (E), *Catalpa bignonioides* 'Aurea', *Chamaecyparis lawsoniana* 'Lanei' (E), *Corylus avellana* 'Aurea', *Cupressus macrocarpa* 'Goldcrest' (E), *Gleditsia triacanthos* 'Sunburst', *Ligustrum ovalifolium* 'Aureum' (E), *Philadelphus coronarius* 'Aureus', *Robinia pseudoacacia* 'Frisia', *Sambucus racemosa* 'Plumosa Aurea', *Spiraea × bumalda* 'Goldflame', and *Spiraea japonica* 'Golden Princess'.

VARIEGATED SHRUBS/TREES *Acer negundo* 'Variegatum', *Cornus alba* 'Elegantissima', *Elaeagnus pungens* 'Maculata' (E), *Euonymus fortunei* 'Emerald 'n' Gold' (E,S), *Hebe × andersonii* 'Variegata' (E), *Hedera canariensis* 'Gloire de Marengo' (E,S), *Hedera colchica* 'Dentata Variegata' (E,S), *Hedera helix* 'Goldheart' (E,S), *Ilex × altaclarensis* 'Golden King' (E,S), *Salvia officinalis* 'Icterina' (E), and *Weigela florida* 'Variegata'.

SILVER/GREY SHRUBS *Artemisia absinthium* (E), *Artemisia schmidtiana* (E), *Ballota pseudodictamnus* (E), *Convolvulus cneorum* (E), *Hebe*

ABOVE *Philadelphus coronarius* 'Aureus' is one of the most popular golden-leaved shrubs.

RIGHT Equally popular for its purple leaves is *Cotinus coggygria* 'Foliis Purpureis'.

pinguifolia 'Pagei' (E), *Helichrysum splendidum* (E), *Helichrysum petiolatum* (E), *Lavandula angustifolia* 'Grappenhall' (E), *Pyrus salicifolia* 'Pendula' (small tree), *Ruta graveolens* 'Jackman's Blue' (E), *Santolina chamaecyparissus* (E), and *Senecio* 'Sunshine' (E).

RED/PURPLE PERENNIALS *Bergenia cordifolia* 'Purpurea' (S,E), *Ophiopogon planiscapus* 'Nigrescens' (black foliage, E), *Rheum palmatum* 'Atrosanguineum', and *Sedum spathulifolium* 'Purpureum' (E).

GOLDEN PERENNIALS *Chrysanthemum parthenium* 'Aureum' (E), hostas in variety (S), *Humulus lupulus* 'Aureus' (climber), *Milium effusum* 'Aureum' (grass), *Valeriana phu* 'Aurea'.

VARIEGATED PERENNIALS *Hosta* in variety (S), *Iris pallida* 'Variegata' (E), *Molinia caerulea* 'Variegata' (grass), *Phalaris arundinacea* 'Picta' (grass), *Phormium* in variety (E).

SILVER/GREY PERENNIALS *Anaphalis triplinervis, Artemisia ludoviciana, Avena candida* (grass, E), *Festuca glauca* (grass, E), *Lamium maculatum* 'Beacon Silver' (E), *Raoulia australis* (E), and *Stachys lanata* 'Silver Carpet' (E).

Autumn leaf colour In every garden there should be plenty of shrubs, and perhaps a few trees, for autumn leaf colour – those which produce brilliant reds, scarlet, crimson, orange, flame shades and deep golds. The shrubs combine marvellously with autumn flowers, such as perennial asters (Michaelmas daisies) and sedums, and with shrubs noted for their colourful berries (see page 28).

As with so many plants, those noted for autumn leaf colour need a dark background so their colours show up really well. I particularly favour dark conifers (especially pines if you have the space to grow them).

Otherwise use more restrained shrubs such as *Viburnum tinus*.

SOME PLEASING PLANT GROUPS
• A background of the dark green *Pinus cembra* (Arolla pine), with *Acer palmatum* varieties, or *Acer capillipes*, in front. Perhaps a graceful birch (*Betula*) with white bark (see page 24).
• *Cotinus coggygria* 'Flame' (brilliant flame colours) with a group of pampas grass (*Cortaderia selloana* 'Pumila' or 'Sunningdale Silver'), which will still be in flower.
• To brighten up a wall or fence try *Vitis coignetiae* (scarlet and orange autumn colour) and the cream and green variegated ivy, *Hedera colchica* 'Dentata Variegata'.
• If you are lucky enough to have a woodland area, try planting an acer glade, using varieties of *Acer palmatum* and/or *Acer japonicum*. Otherwise plant one or two in a mixed shrub border.

TREES FOR AUTUMN COLOUR *Acer capillipes* (red tints), *Crataegus prunifolia* (orange and scarlet), *Liquidambar styraciflua* (crimson and purple), *Malus tschonoskii* (red and gold), *Nyssa sylvatica* (red, yellow and orange; needs acid soil), *Parrotia persica* (crimson and gold).

SHRUBS FOR AUTUMN COLOUR *Acer japonicum* and varieties (red or crimson), *Acer palmatum* varieties (red, crimson or flame), *Berberis thunbergii* (brilliant red), *Cotinus coggygria* 'Flame' (brilliant orange), *Parthenocissus quinquefolia* (tall climber; brilliant orange and scarlet), *Rhododendron luteum* (orange, crimson and purple), *Rhus typhina* (scarlet, red, orange and yellow), *Viburnum opulus* (red and yellow), *Vitis coignetiae* (climber; brilliant crimson and scarlet).

COLOURFUL STEMS

Trees and shrubs with colourful or interesting bark can be used like foliage trees and shrubs to help form the garden's permanent, living framework. I am rather surprised that we see so little use made of plants with coloured bark in private gardens. We may see the odd shrubby dogwood or cornus with red or yellow stems, and perhaps a silver birch or two, but little else from the wide range available.

There are few better plants for winter colour in the garden than those with coloured bark and they associate particularly well with winter-flowering plants such as hamamelis or witch hazels, winter sweet or chimonanthus, the Cornelian cherry (*Cornus mas*), winter-flowering heathers (*Erica herbacea* and *Erica × darleyensis* varieties), *Prunus subhirtella* 'Autumnalis', the evergreen mahonias and *Viburnum tinus*.

Some look particularly pleasing near a pool, such as the red-stemmed salix or willows and the shrubby cornus, as well as *Taxodium distichum*, the swamp cypress. Others are superb in light woodland, like the acers listed here and on page 22, *Betula* (birches) and *Prunus serrula*. Failing such ideal conditions, try them as specimen trees in a lawn where their attractive stems should be shown to advantage.

Plants with outstanding bark:
Acer hersii This is one of the snake-bark maples, so called because the bark resembles a snake's skin. It is a small tree, ideal for a small to average garden, and its trunk and branches are green, conspicuously striped with white. As a bonus, the leaves take on red autumn tints.
Acer palmatum 'Senkaki' This large shrub is popularly known as the coral bark maple because its young branches and twigs are bright coral-red, showing up particularly well in winter when the leaves have fallen, but

ABOVE Several of the birches have beautiful white bark and one of the best is *Betula jacquemontii*, which is a suitable choice for gardens of medium size. It needs a dark background such as deep green foliage shrubs to show it up.

RIGHT Snake-bark maples have bark which resembles a snake's skin. The trunk and branches are green, conspicuously striped with white. Most of the maples also have good leaf colour in the autumn.

not before they have turned soft yellow in autumn.

Betula Several of the birches have beautiful silver or white bark. One of the best, *Betula jacquemontii*, is described on page 46. Others worth growing are *B. ermanii*, with creamy white bark which peels, often tinted with pink, and orange-brown branches, a large tree; *B.* 'Jermyns', a medium tree with creamy-white bark on the trunk but orange-brown on the branches. *B. papyrifera*, the paper birch, a large tree with brilliant white papery bark, and *B. pen-dula*, the common silver birch, a medium-sized tree with rough white bark. All marvellous trees which look particularly good with autumn-colouring trees and shrubs, and with rhododendrons and heathers.

Cornus alba This is the red-barked dogwood, a medium-sized shrub which is best pruned almost to the ground in early spring each year to obtain the best colour. It forms thickets of red stems. Varieties (all best hard pruned) include 'Kesselringii' with purplish black bark and 'Sibirica' (see page 46).

Cornus stolonifera 'Flaviramea' Of similar habit to above, again best hard pruned in early spring, but with deep yellow young shoots. All the shrubby cornus love wet soils and look particularly good by a pool.

Cryptomeria japonica This is a large coniferous tree (the Japanese cedar), with most attractive reddish brown bark which peels off in strips. Only suitable for large gardens.

Eucalyptus gunnii The most widely grown eucalyptus in the U.K., eventually making a large tree, but can be kept as a shrub by hard pruning in early spring each year. However, if you cut it hard you will not get the full beauty of the bark, though its silver-blue juvenile leaves make it an excellent foliage plant. When grown as a tree the bark is at first pale green or cream, but later turns grey or greyish brown.

Metasequoia glyptostroboides This is the dawn redwood, a large tree and a deciduous conifer with orange or reddish-brown bark which peels off.

Prunus serrula Quite unlike most other ornamental cherries, the trunk and branches of this small tree look like polished mahogany, being glossy and reddish brown. An excellent tree for woodland or as a lawn specimen. It produces white flowers in spring.

Rubus It may come as a surprise to many people to learn that some of the brambles have beautiful bark. *Rubus cockburnianus*, a medium-sized shrub, has an arching habit of growth, with its purple stems thickly covered in a white waxy 'bloom'. *R. thibetanus*, or its variety 'Silver Fern', is another medium-sized shrub with a purple-brown bark covered in blue-white 'bloom'. Both these brambles are best cut back hard in early spring each year to encourage plenty of young shoots, which have the best colour.

Salix alba varieties. Some of the varieties of the white willow have highly coloured bark, like the scarlet willow, *S. alba* 'Chermesina', described on page 47. *S. alba* 'Vitellina',

Many of the eucalyptus have colourful patchwork bark. This is the snow gum (*Eucalyptus niphophila*), not quite as hardy as the better-known *E. gunnii*.

ABOVE AND RIGHT The scarlet willow, *Salix alba* 'Chermesina', has brilliant bark which shows up particularly well in winter. It should be grown as a shrub by cutting it back hard annually in early spring. This encourages new young shoots to sustain the good colour.

the golden willow, is also well worth growing, as it has bright, deep yellow young shoots. These willows would eventually make large trees, but are best grown as shrubs, as their young shoots display the best colour. Therefore, in early spring each year, cut them down to 30-90cm (1-3ft) from the ground. The stumps will send up thickets of new shoots. *S. daphnoides*, the violet willow, with purple shoots covered with white 'bloom', can be treated in the same way.

Taxodium distichum This is the swamp cypress, a large deciduous conifer with soft, shredding, reddish brown bark, ideal beside a pool or lake in large gardens.

Dead stems This may seem an odd suggestion, but the dead stems of some plants can look most attractive in winter. Ornamental grasses, for instance, take on creamy, buff or beige tones when dead, so postpone cutting them back until early spring. The almost transparent seed pods of honesty (*Lunaria biennis*) are silvery and well worth keeping.

BERRIES AND FRUITS

Like foliage and coloured-stemmed trees and shrubs, the plants noted for their colourful autumn berries and fruits are invaluable for their contribution to the garden's living framework. Berrying and fruiting trees often make beautiful lawn specimens, while berrying shrubs are ideal for mixed or shrub borders, associating particularly well with others noted for autumn leaf colour, and with such autumn flowers as Michaelmas daisies or asters, dahlias and chrysanthemums.

One of the great problems with berrying trees and shrubs is their attractiveness to birds. They will strip the berries from some shrubs and trees even before they are fully ripe, especially in country gardens. Wherever possible I have selected plants which the birds leave alone, but to make a representative list I have had to include some which are likely to provide bird food instead of garden colour in some areas. Many of the sorbus or mountain ashes, cotoneasters and pyracanthas are particularly prone to birds.

Some of the plants described here are climbers, which will add interest to walls and fences, or could be trained up quite large trees.

Berries and fruits come in a wide range of colours – so I have split my selection into colour groups for easy reference.

Red berried

Arbutus unedo A small tree, popularly known as the Killarney strawberry tree, with white flowers and reddish orange strawberry-like fruits. This evergreen tree's bark is a rich, reddish brown.

Aucuba japonica Medium-sized evergreen shrub with red berries. Plant male and female forms to obtain berries. 'Salicifolia' is a good female form for berries, and 'Crotonifolia' an attractive male form that has gold-speckled leaves.

Berberis hybrids There are many barberry hybrids with attractive berries, making small to medium-sized shrubs. Select from 'Barbarossa', 'Bountiful', 'Buccaneer', 'Pirate King' (see page 44) and *B. × rubrostilla*.

Celastrus orbiculatus A vigorous climber which has red and yellow seed heads in autumn. Plant male and female forms, or a hermaphrodite form for berries. Good clear yellow autumn leaf colour.

Cotoneaster Many to choose from here, including *C. bullatus floribundus* (medium shrub), *C. conspicuus* 'Decorus' (dwarf shrub), 'Coral Beauty' (dwarf shrub), 'Cornubia' (see page 44), *C. frigidus* (large shrub), *C.*

LEFT The Killarney strawberry tree, *Arbutus unedo*, has strawberry-like fruits which appear with the flowers.

RIGHT There are several varieties of *Pernettya mucronata* which have large berries in various colours such as pink and red.

horizontalis (prostrate shrub), *'Hybridus Pendulas'* (generally grown as a standard, when it weeps), *C. microphyllus* (dwarf shrub), *C. salicifolius* 'Autumn Fire' (small shrub), *C. salicifolius* 'Parkteppich' (dwarf shrub), *C. salicifolius* 'Repens' (dwarf shrub), *C. simonsii* (medium shrub), 'Skogholm' (dwarf shrub), and *C. splendens* 'Sabrina' (medium shrub). The dwarf kinds make excellent ground cover.

Euonymus europaeus 'Red Cascade' A variety of the spindle, a medium-sized shrub with masses of red fruits in the autumn, and brilliant autumn leaf colour.

Ilex aquifolium 'J.C. van Tol' There are lots of hollies to choose from but this variety is very free fruiting. It's a large evergreen shrub.

Pernettya mucronata A dwarf evergreen shrub for acid soils. Many varieties, but highly recommended for its free-fruiting habit is 'Bell's Seedling' with large deep red berries. It's hermaphrodite, so a single plant will produce berries.

LEFT *Rosa moyesii* is a medium-sized species of shrub rose with large bottle-shaped fruits following its crimson blooms.

RIGHT Although not often thought of as a berrying shrub, the laurustinus or *Viburnum tinus* has attractive fruits.

Rosa moyesii A medium-sized species of shrub rose with large bottle-shaped fruits, following its crimson flowers. Variety 'Geranium' is popular, with larger fruits.

Skimmia Small or dwarf evergreen shrubs. If you grow *S. japonica* varieties you will need male and female plants for berries, such as 'Foremanii' (female) and 'Fragrans' (male). *S. reevesiana* is hermaphrodite so only one plant is needed for berries.

Stranvaesia davidiana A large evergreen shrub of vigorous habit, something like a cotoneaster. Masses of crimson fruits in large clusters.

Viburnum betulifolium A large shrub with huge clusters of pendulous translucent red berries. Best to grow several plants in a group to ensure a good crop of berries.

Pink berried

Sorbus vilmorinii A small tree with pendulous clusters of deep pink berries. The leaves turn red and purple in the autumn before they fall.

Orange berried

Malus 'John Downie' One of the ornamental crab apples, a small tree bearing heavy crops of edible, bright orange, red-flushed fruits.

Hippophae rhamnoides The sea buckthorn, a medium-sized shrub, the females of which produce masses of orange berries which last all winter. Plant in groups of males and females to ensure berries.

Pyracantha There are many firethorns to choose from, all medium to large shrubs, such as *P. coccinea* 'Lalandei', 'Mohave', 'Orange Charmer', Orange Glow (see page 44), and 'Soleil d'Or'. Pyracanthas are very amenable to training on walls or fences and can also be used as hedging, but the harder they are pruned the fewer berries will be produced.

Yellow berried

Cotoneaster Several cotoneasters have yellow berries, such as 'Exburiensis' (large shrub), 'Pink Champagne' (large shrub, berries become pink tinged later), and 'Rothschild-

ianus' (a large shrub with cream-yellow berries).

Ilex aquifolium 'Bacciflava' The yellow-fruited holly, a large evergreen shrub with masses of bright yellow berries. Another good yellow-berried holly is *I. a.* 'Pyramidalis Fructuluteo', a medium-sized tree with bright yellow berries.

Pyracantha There are a few yellow-berried firethorns, such as 'Buttercup' (a medium-sized shrub, and *P. rogersiana* 'Flava' (a large shrub).

Sorbus aucuparia 'Xanthocarpa' Yellow-berried form of the mountain ash, a most attractive small tree.·

White berried

Sorbus hupehensis A small tree with pendulous clusters of white berries, often lightly tinted with pink. These last well into the winter.

Symphoricarpos rivularis The ever-popular snowberry, a medium-sized shrub which forms dense thickets of growth. Large round brilliant white berries are produced in autumn.

Blue/Purple berried

Callicarpa bodinieri giraldii A medium-sized shrub which freely produces dark lilac berries if several plants are set in a group. A fairly recent introduction is *C. b.* 'Profusion', with purple-blue berries, very freely produced.

Gaultheria shallon A medium-sized evergreen shrub that is a good choice for acid soils, and has large deep purple berries.

Vitis 'Brant' A popular hardy grape vine with purple-black edible fruits in autumn, and reasonably good autumn leaf colour.

OTHER FORMS OF COLOUR

Colour does not only come from green lawns, bright flower beds, shrubs and trees. Various artificial features also provide colour. These include brick paths and walls, wooden fencing and trellis of all kinds, gravel paths, any garden ornaments, the rocks in a rock garden if there is one and, of course, many kinds of garden furniture.

Brickwork Bricks come in many colours, including all shades of red, yellow and even black. When using brickwork in the garden, for walls and perhaps paths, why not try to match them with those of your house? Don't dismiss the possibility of obtaining old weathered bricks, which can look most attractive in a cottage-style garden, for instance. But don't use them for paths – buy hard paving bricks. Remember that brick walls can be painted – perhaps a useful way of brightening up a basement garden, or a small enclosed backyard. Use masonry paint, in white, cream or pale grey. A large mirror skilfully mounted on a wall in a basement or very tiny garden, can give the illusion of extra space.

Trellis and fencing Free-standing trelliswork screens make attractive garden features, and can be regularly treated with a coloured horticultural wood preservative – say red cedar or dark oak – or painted white or pale grey. Timber fencing, such as lapped panels or close-boarded, probably looks best treated with a coloured wood preservative, though modern ranch-type fencing and traditional picket fences look good when painted a crisp white.

Paving slabs There is no doubt that natural-stone paving, such as York stone with its mellow buff tones, looks good in any garden. However, many of the artificial concrete paving slabs in natural-stone colours look almost as good. You can buy coloured slabs, but I suggest you avoid really strong colours as some do not blend in too well in gardens. Go for buff, beige, fawn, or perhaps pale grey shades.

Gravel and pebbles Gravelled areas provide another texture in a garden and though it is possible to buy coloured gravels, the natural ones look more pleasing. Pinkish gravel, though, has it uses, particularly in modern settings, and grey gravel can form an excellent background for colourful plants. Pebbles are also used to cover areas of ground and again come in fairly neutral colours as well as pink and grey. Cobbles used as a hard surface contrast well with paving, both in texture and colour. Some are dark while others are lighter coloured.

Natural rock This is used mainly for building rock gardens, though also for constructing dry-stone walls. It is best to use local rock as it is more in keeping with the area. In your area it could be sandstone, often a beautiful honey colour, or white limestone, or even a more subtle 'blue' or grey slate.

LEFT Many concrete paving slabs are available in natural-stone colours which are a better choice than highly coloured slabs; these can be overwhelming.

TOP A bronze statue in a white and silver garden.

RIGHT This blue glazed container gives an oriental atmosphere.

A grey stone trough in classical style contrasts superbly with these pink and red ivy-leaved pelargoniums.

Ornaments Urns, pots and tubs come in various colours. Terracotta clay is a lovely warm orangey colour, while simulated-stone containers are pale buff or fawn shades, or perhaps white. Wooden tubs can be treated with coloured horticultural wood preservative (perhaps dark oak), or painted white, grey or brown. Widowboxes could be painted to match or complement the colour of the window frames.

Statues can add style to a garden and are generally used as focal points, to lead the eye to a particular part of the garden. All kinds of figures are obtainable, from human forms to animals and birds. Some are in simulated stone, and can be white or buff; others, more expensive, are made of bronze (or bronze coloured) or of lead.

Garden furniture A tremendous range of furniture is available suitable for garden use, from timber tables and chairs, perhaps in teak, oak or red cedar, which are best treated regularly with oil or wood preservative, to tables and chairs in white plastic-coated aluminium or steel, in both traditional and modern designs (the former resembling wrought-iron). White furniture looks particularly attractive on a patio, perhaps accompanied by colourful sunshades and cushions.

Garden buildings These buildings should, I feel sure, blend in with the garden. Summerhouses, for instance, are built of timber and should be treated with appropriate coloured wood preservative. Greenhouses and conservatories have become more 'colourful' in recent years. For instance, some of the aluminium-framed models have an acrylic or anodised finish. The bronze finish blends in beautifully with gardens. White conservatories are exceedingly smart and go with modern or older-style houses. Greenhouses in western red cedar harmonize with the garden. I think I would avoid raw aluminium greenhouses in the ornamental part of the garden as they do not blend in so well – too strong a contrast.

Timber decking This idea has come from America and is used in place of paving slabs, concrete, etc., to construct areas for sitting and entertaining. And very good it looks, too: generally stained a dark brown, it is a natural choice for gardens.

ABOVE Cane furniture is a particularly good choice for a conservatory as it blends so well with plants.

LEFT White is the traditional colour of greenhouses and it does not by any means look out of place in a garden. Remember that a greenhouse can be partially hidden by plants but have a care not to obstruct light from entering it.

SEASONAL COLOUR

My aim here is to show that you can enjoy colour from plants all through the year. Why so many gardens are devoid of colour in winter I do not know, for there are many suitable plants to choose from. Indeed, the entire list represents only a fraction of those available for each season of the year. But they have been chosen on their merits – they are among the very best garden plants available.

The list has been divided into spring, summer, autumn and winter, and each season contains a selection of perennials, shrubs and trees. Some are noted for flowers, others for coloured foliage, coloured stems, berries or autumn leaf colour.

SPRING
Perennials
Bergenia
(Pig-squeak) Dwarf perennials, all worth growing for their early blooms in shades of red, pink or white, which show up well against the large, leathery, shiny leaves. Ideal plants for shady spots and moist soil, although highly adaptable to other sites.

Dicentra spectabilis
(Bleeding heart) A dwarf perennial for shade and moist soil, producing sprays of rosy-red flowers with white hips in late spring and early summer. The ferny foliage is attractive, too. A delightful white-flowered form is also available and well worth searching for.

Doronicum
(Leopard's bane) An indispensable dwarf perennial with yellow daisy flowers. Good varieties are 'Miss Mason' and the deep yellow, fully double-flowered 'Spring Beauty'. Provide good drainage and sun, but otherwise this little plant is very easy going.

Euphorbia epithymoides
(Spurge) Another excellent dwarf perennial for early blooms, which are acid yellow. It likes sun and moist yet well-drained soil.

Primula denticulata
(Drumstick primrose) My favourite primula, very easily grown in moist soil and shade or partial shade. It produces globular mauve (or white) flower heads on 30cm (1ft) high stems, grows vigorously and increases rapidly.

Shrubs and trees
Berberis darwinii
(Barberry) A medium-sized evergreen shrub with small holly-like leaves, this is one of the most popular barberries, with deep golden flowers in spring. Full sun and well-drained soil needed for best results.

Chaenomeles superba
'Firedance' (Ornamental quince) A medium-sized shrub grown for its glowing red single rose-like flowers. It needs good drainage and a position in sun or partial shade.

Several euphorbias or spurges flower in spring or early summer. Here's an attractive combination of a lime-green spurge with *E. griffithii* 'Fireglow'.

LEFT A classical spring combination of bedding tulips and myosotis or forget-me-nots.

BELOW *Pieris formosa forrestii* is noted for its brilliant red young leaves in the spring. Unfortunately it will only grow in acid soil.

Choisya ternata
(Mexican orange blossom) A medium-sized evergreen shrub noted for its masses of scented white flowers over a very long period. Provide sun, good drainage and shelter from cold winds.

Forsythia
'Lynwood' (Golden bells) No garden is complete without forsythia, which makes a magnificent show of bright yellow blooms. 'Lynwood' is undoubtedly the best, with masses of large blooms. A medium-sized shrub; likes sun and good drainage.

Pieris formosa forrestii
A large evergreen shrub for acid soils and partial shade, which is grown as much for its brilliant red young leaves as for its long trusses of scented white spring flowers. A good form is 'Wakehurst' with brilliant red young foliage.

Prunus
'Amanogawa' (Ornamental cherry) Ornamental cherries are the very essence of spring, but most are too large for many gardens. Not so 'Amanogawa' which forms a slim column, clothed with pink blossoms. Needs a sunny, well-drained spot.

Viburnum tinus
(Laurustinus) An extremely useful medium to large shrub, with deep green evergreen leaves and masses of white flowers in the late winter or spring. An excellent variety is 'Eve Price' with carmine flower buds. Grows in full sun or partial shade and any well-drained soil. A good choice on chalk.

SUMMER
Perennials
Campanula lactiflora
(Bellflower) A 90cm (3ft) high perennial with lavender-blue bell-shaped blooms, ideal for a 'blue border'. Grows in sun or partial shade and any moist but well-drained soil.

Festuca glauca
(Fescue grass) A dwarf blue-grey grass which has many uses as a foliage plant. It is evergreen, needs good drainage, and a sunny position for best colour.

Hemerocallis
(Day lily) The day lilies are invaluable for their exceedingly long season of flowering – continuing well into autumn. The grassy foliage is attractive, too. There are dozens of varieties in many colours – something for all colour schemes. Provide well-drained yet moist soil, and a position in sun or partial shade.

Hosta sieboldiana
'Elegans' (Plantain lily) The hostas are low-growing foliage plants, though they do produce lilac or white blooms in summer. Some have variegated foliage, others golden, yet others greyish or bluish, like 'Elegans', with very large bluish leaves. Hostas need moist soil and are ideal for cool shady spots.

LEFT The blue-grey fescue grass, *Festuca* 'Glauca', is evergreen and happily combines with many other plants. Needs full sun for best colour.

BELOW The day lilies have a remarkably long season of flowering and the lily-like blooms come in a wide range of pastel and strong colours.

The border phloxes are indispensable border plants, flowering for a long period. They come in a wide range of strong and pastel colours.

Phlox paniculata
(Border phlox) Like the day lilies, the phloxes are indispensable border plants, flowering for a long period. There are many colours to choose from so they can be incorporated into any colour scheme. They are of medium height, like good drainage yet moist soil, and thrive in sun or partial shade.

Shrubs and trees
Acer negundo
'Variegatum' (Box elder) A medium-sized deciduous foliage tree with light green leaves boldly edged white, giving overall a very light effect. Very adaptable, for sun or partial shade.

Buddleia davidii
(Butterfly bush) Medium-sized shrub grown for its long spikes of flowers in various colours. 'Royal Red' is very popular, with red-purple blooms. Grows in any soil but likes full sun.

Cotinus coggygria
'Royal Purple' (Smoke tree) Distinguished for its lovely, plume-like inflorescences and one of the best purple-leaved shrubs, it makes a large, freely-branching specimen but can be kept smaller by careful pruning. Grows in any well-drained soil and either in full sun or partial shade.

Escallonia
Small or medium-sized evergreen shrubs grown for their flowers, in shades of red, pink or white carried over a long period. Any of the 'Donard' varieties are well worth growing. Any well-drained soil in full sun is suitable.

Gleditsia triacanthos
'Sunburst' (Honey locust) One of the best medium-sized golden trees, with bright yellow young foliage. Give it a site in full sun for the best colour and a well-drained soil. An excellent choice for town gardens.

Philadelphus
(Mock orange) Popular small or medium-sized shrubs with white flowers in early summer often heavily scented. Well-known varieties are 'Beauclerk', 'Belle Etoile' and 'Virginal'. Provide full sun but any soil is suitable.

Philadelphus coronarius
'Aureus' (Golden mock orange) One of the most popular golden-foliage shrubs for a position in full sun. A medium-sized shrub.

Pyrus salicifolia
'Pendula' (Willow-leaved pear) A small weeping tree with silvery grey willow-like leaves. Makes a beautiful lawn specimen, or a background for brightly coloured flowers. Good drainage and sun needed.

Robinia pseudoacacia
'Frisia' (False acacia) A small to medium-sized tree with deep golden foliage, the colour lasting well right through to autumn. Full sun and good drainage.

AUTUMN
Perennials
Anemone × hybrida
(Japanese anemone) Late-flowering short to medium perennial, which blooms for a long period. Colours are white or shades of pink. Among the best varieties are 'Bressingham Glow' (rose-pink) and 'September Charm' (soft pink). Takes partial shade. Good on chalk soils.

Aster novi-belgii varieties
(Michaelmas daisies) These dwarf to medium-height perennials represent the very essence of autumn. There are many varieties in shades of red, pink, blue, purple and so on. Full sun and good drainage.

Nerine bowdenii
A bulbous plant which produces pink flowers in late autumn up to 60cm (24in) high. Plant in full sun in a sheltered, well-drained spot.

Schizostylis coccinea
(Kaffir lily) Growing about 60cm (2ft) high, this perennial has grassy

A good white variety of *Anemone × hybrida* or Japanese anemone is 'Louise Uhink'. Excellent for chalky soils and for partial shade.

LEFT Michaelmas daisies represent the very essence of autumn. There are dwarf and medium-height varieties in many colours.

BELOW *Schizostylis coccinea* 'Major', one of the Kaffir lilies, needs a position in full sun and very good drainage.

foliage and deep red flowers in variety 'Major' and clear pink in the well-known 'Mrs Hegarty'. Needs full sun, very good, sharp drainage and a well sheltered spot.

Sedum spectabile

(Stonecrop) Dwarf perennial with flat heads of flowers over a long period, light pink in the species, and salmon-pink in variety 'Autumn Joy'. Provide full sun and well-drained soil.

Shrubs and trees

Acer palmatum

(Japanese maple) Marvellous small, medium or large shrubs, depending on variety, for autumn leaf colour. Provide a sheltered spot and partial shade. The Dissectum varieties have ferny leaves, while the Heptalobum group has deeply lobed leaves. One of the best is 'Heptalobum Osakazuki' whose leaves turn a brilliant flame colour in autumn.

Berberis
'Pirate King' (Barberry) Many barberries have colourful autumn berries, but this is one of the best with
orange-red berries in profusion. It's a
small, very adaptable shrub, taking
partial shade.

Cotinus coggygria
'Flame' (Smoke tree) The best variety of the smoke tree for autumn leaf
colour — its foliage turns brilliant
orange. It makes a large shrub but
can be pruned back. Grow in sun and
well-drained soil.

Cotoneaster
'Cornubia' This is one of the best for
autumn berries. It makes a large
evergreen shrub loaded down with
large red berries. Adaptable and
good for chalk soils.

Malus
'Golden Hornet' (Ornamental crab
apple) A small tree with bright yellow (edible) fruits which hang on the
tree for a very long time. Very adaptable but best in a sunny well-drained
spot. Makes a good lawn specimen.

Malus tschonoskii
(Ornamental crab apple) A medium-
sized tree grown for its autumn leaf
colour — brilliant reddish orange. It
has white flowers, followed by yel-
low-green fruits, and a compact con-
ical habit.

Pyracantha
'Orange Glow' (Firethorn) A large
evergreen shrub laden in autumn
with brilliant orange-red berries.
Very adaptable as regards soils and
situation, taking shade as well as full
sun. The berries last well into winter.

Rhus typhina
(Stag's-horn sumach) A large sucker-
ing shrub with compound leaves

which turn brilliant shades of
orange, red, scarlet and yellow in autumn. Very adaptable but needs
plenty of sun for best results.

Sorbus
'Joseph Rock' (Mountain ash) A
small tree of upright, compact habit,
at its best in autumn when it carries
yellow berries and has bright red and
orange leaf colour. Makes an excellent lawn specimen.

TOP *Cotinus*
coggygria, the smoke
tree, in full flower. It is
also noted for its
brilliant autumn leaf
colour. A large shrub
which can be pruned.

ABOVE *Sorbus*
'Joseph Rock' is a
small tree of compact
habit, ideal for limited
space. The yellow
berries hang on the
tree for a long time.

WINTER
Perennials
Helleborus niger
(Christmas rose) Dwarf evergreen perennial with large white single-rose-like flowers – one always hopes at Christmas time, though they may appear later. 'Potter's Wheel' is a good variety. Takes partial shade and likes a moist rich soil.

Helleborus orientalis
(Lenten rose) Dwarf evergreen perennial flowering in late winter, over a very long period. Many named forms available with flowers in red, pink, purple, cream or white shades. Suited to partial or dappled shade and moist soil.

Iris unguicularis
(Winter-flowering iris) A dwarf perennial with grassy evergreen foliage and a long succession of lavender-blue flowers. Variety 'Mrs Barnard' has larger blooms, more freely produced. Needs a warm spot and very good drainage.

Shrubs and trees
Acer davidii
(Snake bark maple) A small tree with green and white striated bark. Autumn leaf tints are a bonus. An ideal tree for light woodland, shrub border or lawn.

Acer griseum
(Paperbark maple) Same uses as A. davidii, but totally different in habit. Its papery reddish-brown bark peels off, revealing bright reddish brown underbark. The autumn leaf colour is superb. A small, compact tree.

A variety of Lenten rose, *Helleborus orientalis*. These are dwarf evergreen perennials which are suited to partial or dappled shade and moist soil.

LEFT *Betula jacquemontii* is a medium-sized tree and certainly one of the best birches for stem colour. It needs a dark background to show it up.

RIGHT The witch hazel, *Hamamelis mollis* 'Pallida', is a large spreading shrub but is slow growing.

Betula jacquemontii
(Birch) A medium-sized tree and certainly one of the best birches for stem colour. The bark is brilliant white and peels off. Superb lawn specimen also ideal for light woodland or a shrub border. Suited to moist soils.

Calluna vulgaris
'Gold Haze' The golden-leaved heathers really come into their own in winter. Good ground cover, needing acid soil and full sun.

Chamaecyparis lawsoniana
'Lanei' (Lawson cypress) Many conifers have golden foliage, but this one is very highly rated. The golden-yellow foliage is carried in feathery sprays. A medium-sized cone-shaped tree for full sun and moist, yet well-drained soil.

Chaemaecyparis pisifera
'Boulevard' (Sawara cypress) One of the dwarf conifers – must be the most popular of those with grey-blue foliage. Forms a neat broad cone shape. Best in slightly acid soil, and full sun or partial shade.

Cornus alba
'Sibirica' (Westonbirt dogwood) The best of the red-stemmed, shrubby dogwoods, with bright crimson bark. Cut the plant almost to ground level in early spring each year to encourage plenty of new shoots. Ideal for moist soil and especially recommended for poolside planting.

Cornus mas
(Cornelian cherry) A large shrub with yellow flowers on bare twigs. The foliage colours quite well in autumn. Sun or semi-shade.

Elaeagnus pungens
'Maculata' A medium-sized evergreen shrub with large leaves conspicuously splashed in the centre with gold. Adaptable but will not grow too well in shallow chalky soils. Needs plenty of sun.

Erica herbacea (E. carnea)
(Winter-flowering heather). Many varieties of Erica herbacea make colourful ground cover around large shrubs and flower for an exceedingly long time. Many to choose from, like 'Myretoun Ruby' (deep pink), 'Springwood Pink' (clear pink), 'Springwood White' (white), and 'Vivellii' (carmine). Will grow in chalky soils. Open sunny position.

Hamamelis mollis
'Pallida' (Witch hazel) A large spreading shrub producing sulphur-yellow blooms with strap-shaped petals on bare twigs. Bonus of autumn leaf colour. Moist peaty soil, partial or dappled shade. Ideal for a shrub border or woodland garden.

Ilex × altaclarensis
'Golden King' (Holly) One of the best golden hollies, with almost spineless leaves, broadly edged with brilliant gold. A female variety which will produce berries. Adaptable to various soils and takes partial shade. Grows into a large shrub.

Jasminum nudiflorum
(Winter jasmine) Generally grown as a wall shrub. Produces a succession of bright yellow flowers. Adaptable and suitable for shady walls.

Prunus subhirtella
'Autumnalis' (Autumn cherry) A small tree, flowering between late autumn and early spring. Its semi-double flowers are white, but there's also a pale pink form called 'Autumnalis Rosea'. Choose an open position with well-drained soil.

Salix alba
'Chermesina' (Scarlet willow) The young stems are brilliant orange-scarlet, showing up well in winter. Prune hard in early spring each year to encourage a thicket of young stems. Can be pruned as low as 30cm (1ft) from the ground. Suitable for moist soils: best in sunny spot.

Thuja occidentalis
'Rheingold' (Arborvitae) A very popular dwarf conifer with deep golden foliage, darkening in the winter. Forms a broad cone shape. Full sun and well-drained soil.

Viburnum farreri
A medium-sized deciduous shrub valued for its scented white flowers which come from pink buds. Needs a moist yet well-drained soil, and will take partial or dappled shade. Ideal for a shrub border or woodland garden, where its winter flowers bring a welcome touch of colour.

INDEX AND ACKNOWLEDGEMENTS

annuals: by colours
  15, 16, 18
aspect 11
autumn:
  colour for 42-4, **42**,
  43, **44**
  foliage for 23

background 8-9
bark, *see* stems
bedding plants: by
  colours 15, 16, 17,
  18, 19
berries 28-31
bi-coloured flowers 6
birds 28
blue:
  berries 31
  schemes in **14**, 18-
  19, **19**
borders 12, **12**
brickwork 32
bright atmosphere 7,
  7
buildings 35, **35**
bulbs: by colours
  15, 16, 17, 18, 19

clashing colours 9, **9**
climbers 28
colour wheel 10, **10**
complementary
  colours 9-10
containers 13, **33**, 34,
  34
contrasting colours
  10, **11**
cool atmosphere 7, **7**,
  14, **17**

fencing 32
focal point 13, **13**
foliage plants 20-3,
  20, **22**, **23**
  in plant groups
  20-1, **20**, 23
  sun required 21
  uses 20
framework 8-9
fruits 28-31
furniture, garden 34,
  35

gravel 33
green:
  schemes with white
  15-16, **15**
  shades of 8, **8**

harmonizing colours
  10, **11**
hedges 8, 12, 20
Hidcote Garden 7

illusions 12-13

lawn: specimen trees
  24, 28

mirror images 12
mood 6-7

ornaments 34

pale colours 12
paving **32**, 33
pebbles 33
perennials:
  by colours 14,

15-16, 17, 18-19
for foliage 22-3
for seasonal
  colour 38, 40-1,
  42-3, 45
pink:
  berries 30
  schemes with silver
  6, 16-17, **17**
progressive colours
  10
purple berries 31

red:
  berries 28-30
  scheme in 14-15
rock 33

schemes 6-7
screen 13
seasonal colour 36-47
shade: foliage for 21
shrubs:
  for bark 24-7, **27**
  for berries and fruit
  28-31, **29**, **30**,
  31
  by colours 15, 16,
  17, 18, 19
  for foliage 22, 23
  for seasonal colour
  38-9, 41-2, 43-4,
  45-7
silver: schemes with
  pink, **6**, 16-17,
  17
single-colour
  schemes 14-19
site 11

soil 11
spring: colour for
  38-9, **38**, **39**
statuary 13, **33**, 34
stems 24-7
  coloured 8-9
  dead 27
strong colours 12
summer: colour for
  40-2, **40**, **41**
sun: foliage for 21

timber decking 35
trees:
  for bark 24-7, **24**,
  25, **26**, **27**
  for berries and fruit
  28-31, **28**
  for foliage 22, 23
  for seasonal colour
  38-9 41-2, 43-4,
  45-7
  specimen 24, 28
trellis 32

warm atmosphere 6-7
white:
  berries 31
  schemes with
  green 15-16, **15**
  use 9
winter:
  colour for 45-7, **45**,
  46, **47**
  stems and bark for
  24-7

yellow:
  berries 30-1
  schemes in 17, **18**

Picture credits

Steve Bicknell: 13.
Pat Brindley: 7(t,b),27(b),40(t),41.
John Glover: 8,20,25,39(t).
Lyn & Derek Gould: 24,34.
S & O Mathews: 1,4/5,11(t), 12,33(t).
Tania Midgley: 15,21,23,35(t,b),36/7,44(t).
Harry Smith Horticultural Photographic
Collection: 9,11(b),14,16,18,19,27(t),31,39(b),45.
Michael Warren: 6,17,22,26,28,29,30,32,33(b),38,
  40(b),42,43(t,b),44(b),46,47.